SOCCER LEGENDS

Clive Gifford

Crabtree Publishing Company

www.crabtreebooks.com

Ms. Natalie Vigilante

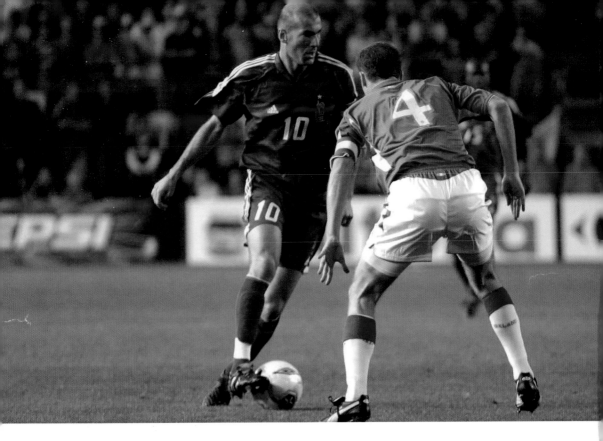

Crabtree Publishing Company

www.crabtreebooks.com   1-800-387-7650

Copyright © **2009 CRABTREE PUBLISHING COMPANY**.

**Published
in Canada
Crabtree Publishing**
616 Welland Ave.
St. Catharines, ON
L2M 5V6

**Published in the
United States
Crabtree Publishing**
PMB 59051
350 Fifth Ave., 59th Floor
New York, NY 10118

Content development by Shakespeare Squared
www.ShakespeareSquared.com

Author: Clive Gifford
Project editor: Ruth Owen
Project designer: Simon Fenn
Photo research: Ruth Owen
Project coordinator: Robert Walker
Production coordinator: Katherine Berti
Prepress technicians: Katherine Berti,
   Ken Wright

Thank you to
Lorraine Petersen
and the members
of nasen

Picture credits:
Corbis: Bernard Bisson/Sygma: p. 23 (inset); Marcus Brandt/epa:
   p. 26–27
Getty Images: p. 13, 28, 29, 31; AFP: front cover, p. 4, 5,
   8–9, 16–17, 18–19, 22–23, 24; Man Utd: p. 10, 11;
   National Geographic: p. 12-13; Popperfoto: p. 6, 7,
   20–21; Bob Thomas: p. 6 (inset), 14–15, 15 (top)
Shutterstock: p. 1, 2–3, 9 (bottom), 10–11 (background). 13 (top),
   16, 24–25 (background), 25 (top), 30–31 (background)

Every effort has been made to trace copyright holders, and we apologize in advance for any omissions. We would be pleased to insert the appropriate acknowledgments in any subsequent edition of this publication.

Library and Archives Canada Cataloguing in Publication

Gifford, Clive
      Soccer legends / Clive Gifford.

(Crabtree contact)
Includes index.
ISBN 978-0-7787-3777-3 (bound).--ISBN 978-0-7787-3799-5 (pbk.)

      1. Soccer players--Biography--Juvenile literature. 2. Soccer--
Juvenile literature. I. Title. II. Series: Crabtree contact

GV942.7.A1G53 2009   j796.334092'2   C2008-907859-4

Printed in the U.S.A./102011/CG20110916

Library of Congress Cataloging-in-Publication Data

Gifford, Clive.
   Soccer legends / Clive Gifford.
      p. cm. -- (Crabtree contact)
   Includes index.
   ISBN 978-0-7787-3799-5 (pbk. : alk. paper) -- ISBN 978-0-
7787-3777-3 (reinforced library binding : alk. paper)
   1. Soccer--Juvenile literature. 2. Soccer players--Juvenile
literature. I. Title. II. Series.

GV943.25.G552 2009
796.3340922--dc22
[B]

                                    2008052388

CONTENTS

GOAL!

Goals win games! This is why soccer's greatest legends are famous for scoring or saving goals.

Brazilian player Rogério Ceni has scored more than 80 goals in his career. Most of the goals were from **free kicks**.

Rogério Ceni

What makes Ceni special?

He's a goalkeeper—the highest scoring ever!

Mia Hamm

Mia Hamm scored an
incredible 158 goals
for the U.S. women's
team. She first played
for her country when
she was 15 years old.

DIXIE DEAN

In 1925, English soccer club Everton signed Dixie Dean. He scored 60 goals in the 1927–28 season. This was a record for the English **league**.

SIR STANLEY MATTHEWS

English soccer star Sir Stanley Matthews began playing in 1932. He retired 33 years later when he was 50. In over 750 matches he did not receive a single **yellow card**.

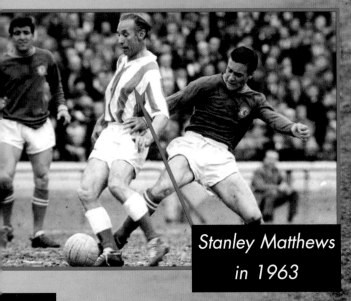

Stanley Matthews in 1963

FERENC PUSKAS

In 1953, Ferenc Puskas masterminded Hungary's 6–3 win against England.

Puskas's powerful left foot scored 83 goals in 84 games for Hungary.

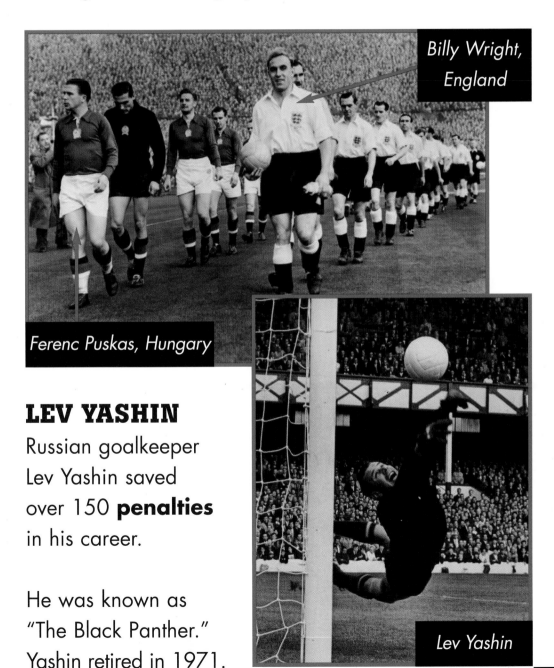

Billy Wright, England

Ferenc Puskas, Hungary

Lev Yashin

LEV YASHIN

Russian goalkeeper Lev Yashin saved over 150 **penalties** in his career.

He was known as "The Black Panther." Yashin retired in 1971.

REAL MADRID

When it comes to legendary soccer clubs, you do not get bigger than Spain's Real Madrid. This team once went 121 home games unbeaten.

In 2008, they won the "La Liga" Spanish League for a record 31st time. They have won the **European Cup/Champions League** nine times.

(Stats at the end of the 2007/08 season.)

At the start of the 21st century, Real Madrid spent big to create a team of superstars. They were known as the "Galacticos."

THE GALACTICOS PRICE TAG

- Zinedine Zidane— $69 million USD
- Luis Figo— $57 million USD
- Ronaldo— $45 million USD
- David Beckham— $38 million USD

MANCHESTER UNITED

Manchester United is England's most famous soccer club. They were first called the Newton Heath Soccer Club in 1878.

TEAM STATS

- 17 English League Championships
- 11 **FA Cups**
- 17 **FA Charity Shields**
- 3 European Cups/ Champions League titles

(Stats at the end of the 2007/08 season.)

Manchester United celebrate winning the 2008 Champions League after a penalty shoot-out.

Man U's boss, Sir Alex Ferguson has managed the club since 1986. In 1998/99, his team won the **Premier League**, the FA Cup, and the Champions League. This is a record for an English club!

2008—Ferguson signs Dimitar Berbatov

TRANSFER FEES

First transfer fee: Gilbert Godsmark for $61.50 USD in 1900.

Bargain buy: Peter Schmeichel (one of the best goalies ever) for $815,190 USD in 1991.

Big money buy: Dimitar Berbatov for $47.3 million USD in 2008.

Strangest fee: Hughie McLenahan for three freezers full of ice cream in 1927.

PELE

Pelé is one of soccer's greatest legends.

Pelé was born into a poor family in Brazil. He shined shoes as a boy to make money. He became the only player to win three World Cup winners medals.

Pelé played for the Brazilian club Santos. He always wore the number 10 shirt. Santos retired the shirt when Pelé retired.

PELE STATS

- Scored 1,284 goals
- Played 92 games for Brazil
- Played over 1,000 games for Brazilian club Santos
- Played over 100 games for New York Cosmos

1974—Pelé leaves the field after his final game for Santos.

DIEGO MARADONA

Maradona was one of Argentina's greatest players. He scored 34 goals for Argentina.

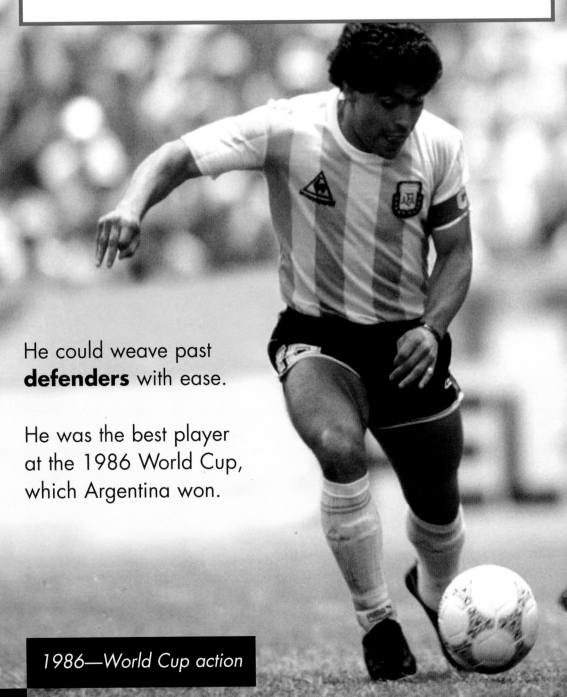

He could weave past **defenders** with ease.

He was the best player at the 1986 World Cup, which Argentina won.

1986—World Cup action

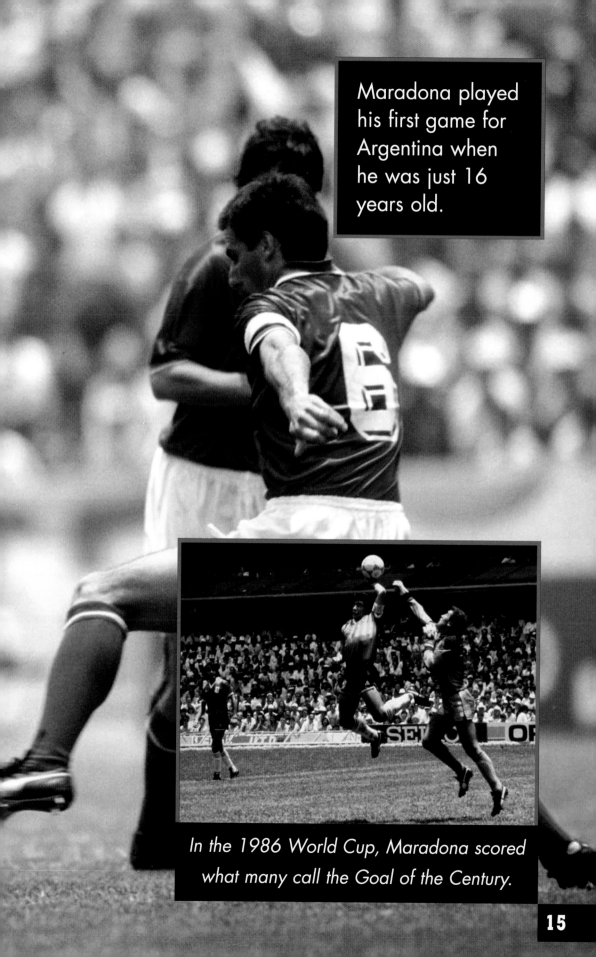

Maradona played his first game for Argentina when he was just 16 years old.

In the 1986 World Cup, Maradona scored what many call the Goal of the Century.

JOHAN CRUYFF

Opponents thought Cruyff was a **center forward**. But he would pop up all over the field!

Cruyff scored 33 goals for the Dutch national team.

CRUYFF WAS THE FIRST PLAYER:

- To be crowned European soccer player of the year three times
- To pass the ball when taking a penalty, receive a pass back, and score
- To have a move named after him. "The Cruyff turn" is a surprise turn that allows a player to shake off an opponent

1974—Cruyff at the World Cup

GIANLUIGI BUFFON

In 2000, Lazio smashed the world record fee for a goalkeeper. They bought Angelo Peruzzi for $17.5 million USD.

Just one year later, Juventus bought Gianluigi Buffon for $49 million USD!

Most fans think he's worth it.

Buffon dives for the ball during training.

AT THE END OF THE 2007/08 SEASON, BUFFON'S MEDALS INCLUDED:

- **UEFA Cup** winner—1999
- Italian **Serie A** League Champion—2002, 2003
- **Italian Super Cup** Winner—1999, 2002, 2003
- Serie A Goalkeeper of the Year—6 times
- World Cup Winner—2006

BOBBY MOORE

In 1966, Bobby Moore, helped England win the World Cup. Moore was a brilliant defender and England's greatest captain.

BOBBY MOORE STATS

- Over 600 games for English club West Ham United
- 108 games for England
- Played 90 games as England captain
- Scored 2 goals for England

" He was my friend as well as the greatest defender I ever played against. "

Pelé

" My captain, my leader, my right-hand man. He was the spirit and the heartbeat of the team. "

England manager, Sir Alf Ramsey

" There should be a law against him. He knows what's happening 20 minutes before everyone else. "

Scotland manager, Jock Stein

ZINEDINE ZIDANE

Zinedine Zidane grew up wanting to be a policeman. Instead, he became the world's most expensive soccer player.

Real Madrid paid over $69 million for Zidane.

Zidane was "FIFA World Player of the Year" three times. He won the World Cup in 1998 with France and the **European Championship** in 2000.

Zidane lost it in the 2006 World Cup Final. He headbutted Italy's Marco Materazzi and was sent off in his last competitive game.

He was still voted the best player of the tournament.

What did Zidane have?
- Touch • **Vision**
- A great pass
- A powerful shot

1998—Zidane scores in the World Cup final against Brazil.

Zidane makes a good pass under pressure.

PAOLO MALDINI

Paolo Maldini is one of the greatest defenders of all time.

Maldini played his first game for AC Milan in 1985. He still plays for the same club today! His father, Cesare, also played for AC Milan.

MALDINI'S RECORD INCLUDES:

- 2007—the oldest player to score in a Champions League final. He was 38 years old.
- 1994—The first defender to win World Soccer magazine's "World Player of the Year" award.

The English Premier League is one of the world's top leagues. However, Maldini refused to leave Milan for another club.

" I have great respect for the Premier League, but why leave Milan? I've got everything I want here. Milan is my family. "

Paolo Maldini

FEMALE LEGENDS

Women's soccer has created its own legends.

Marta Vieira da Silva
Country: Brazil
Club: Umea IK

- Top scorer at 2007 World Cup with 7 goals.
- Scored 47 goals in just 44 games for Brazil.

Many soccer fans say da Silva is the best women's player in the world.

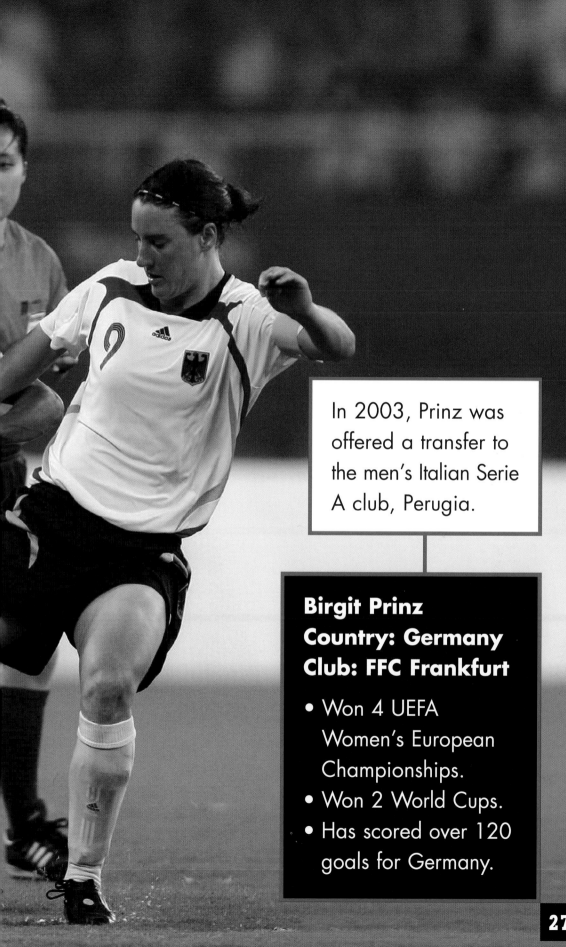

In 2003, Prinz was offered a transfer to the men's Italian Serie A club, Perugia.

Birgit Prinz
Country: Germany
Club: FFC Frankfurt

- Won 4 UEFA Women's European Championships.
- Won 2 World Cups.
- Has scored over 120 goals for Germany.

DAVID BECKHAM

David Beckham is the only team England player to score in three World Cups.

He is one of a small band of players with over 100 England **caps**.

Beckham is famous for his swerving crosses and free kicks.

In August 2008, Beckham was voted "Teen Choice Male Athlete." He beat U.S. superstars from basketball and baseball.

DAVID BECKHAM STATS

- 61 goals for Manchester United
- Only player to be captain for England while playing for a U.S. club (LA Galaxy)
- Only England player to receive two red cards

Three weeks later, Beckham represented the UK at the Closing Ceremony of the Beijing Olympics.

NEED-TO-KNOW WORDS

cap An appearance in the full national soccer team

center forward An attacker who plays closest to the other team's goal

Champions League See European Cup

defender A player whose main role is to stop the other side from scoring goals

European Cup The competition that became the Champions League in the early 1990s. Top league teams from each European country compete for the cup every year

European Championship A competition between the best national teams in Europe. The competition takes place every four years

FA Charity Shield A match played at the start of the English league season. It is usually played between last season's FA Cup winner and the League winners

FA Cup A popular knockout competition for clubs in England and Wales

free kick A kick that restarts the game after a referee has stopped play for offside or a foul

Italian Super Cup A cup competition for the best clubs in Italy

league A group of teams who compete to win a championship. Each team plays all the others in the league at least once

penalty A shot on goal awarded by a referee for a serious foul

Premier League The top level of English club soccer

Serie A The top soccer league in Italy

transfer fee The price paid to move a player from one team to another

UEFA Cup A cup competition for European clubs who finish well in their country's league, but not high enough to enter the Champions League

vision The ability to spot passes and moves that other players are slow to see

yellow card A warning issued by the referee to a player who breaks the rules

ALL-TIME GREATS

- In 1967, two armies which were at war in Nigeria, stopped fighting for 48 hours. Why? To watch Pelé take part in a friendly match!

- Diego Maradona hosted his own television chat show in Argentina. It was called *The Night Of The Number 10*. His guests included Pelé, Zidane, and Ronaldo.

- In 2008, English club West Ham United retired the number 6 shirt in honor of Bobby Moore.

2008—Pelé and David Beckham at a soccer charity event.

SOCCER ONLINE

www.ifhof.com/hof/halloffame.asp

www.planetworldcup.com/LEGENDS/wcstars.html

www.cruijff.com/eng

www.davidbeckham.com

INDEX